Sulcata Tortoise as Pets

The Ultimate Guide for Sulcata Tortoise

General Info, Purchasing, Care, Cost, Keeping, Health, Supplies, Food, Breeding and More Included!

By Lolly Brown

Foreword

Sulcata Tortoise also referred to as African spur thigh tortoise are one of the most popular turtles in the pet trade. They're from hot dry desserts from Central Africa and are very well adapted in very harsh environments. These tortoises have a reputation of being very friendly, inquisitive compared to other turtle or tortoise species, and they also have outgoing personalities. They're not boring pets unlike what we think of most turtles or tortoises and you'll surely enjoy their company for a very long time.

Before you take on the responsibility of getting your first pet tortoise, there are some key facts and important information that you need to know. When taking on a new pet or even for those who already have experience in handling tortoises it's always best to research and study reliable sources like this book!

Table of Contents

Introduction

Tortoises can get very big, many adults can reach over 100 pounds and some can even reach up to 200 pounds! They can also live for a very long time if proper care is given. Some can even outlast their owners, Sulcata Tortoise or also known as African Spur Thighs can live between 70 and 100 years! Taking care of Sulcata tortoises especially when they're still young is quite easy and affordable, but could get quite expensive and time consuming in the long run when they bigger and heavier. As babies and juveniles, sulcata tortoises are quite indoor pets; they can be kept in a smaller enclosure like a ten or twenty gallon tank or terrariums. As they get bigger though, you should purchase a much bigger housing (in all dimensions) because sulcata tortoises or even turtles in general need ample space; even if they are relatively slow they still need to roam around just like any other household pets.

Perhaps one of the fun parts in keeping tortoises is during their growth years because since they are still small, many keepers customize their enclosures; it's popularly known as "tortoise table." Tortoise table are usually set up like sort of a doll house where keepers can contain their cute pets in a wooden box and use some sort of divider or fancy designs for aesthetic purposes. It's super awesome to decorate and your young tortoise will surely have fun exploring their miniature enclosure as well.

In the next few chapters, you'll learn some general information, and biological background as well as the temperament of Sulcata Tortoises. This book will also delve deeper on how to maintain and keep pet tortoises in terms of its health, nutrition, breeding and habitat.

Chapter One: Biological Information

Sulcata tortoises may look very friendly and adorable especially when they are still young, you might even become fond of them and probably think that keeping more than one or two is not enough because after all they are small creatures that you can easily keep and tuck away in a box. They're very easy to maintain and they look really cute which is why you might end up buying a bunch of them. Well, as the saying goes, don't bite more than what you can chew! Don't become an impulse buyer or keeper because they might be low maintenance pets at least for a few months but I can assure you that these tortoises quickly grow and in this chapter you'll find out what they are capable of and their physical traits that will surely stun you.

Sulcata Tortoises in Focus

Sulcata tortoises or African spurred thigh tortoises grow very quickly and can reach 100 pounds in just 10 years! They are one of the largest tortoises in the world – 3rd to be exact coming in after Galapagos and Synchilla tortoises. These tortoises originally came from the Sahara desert in Africa particularly in the southern rim area. They live for a very long time, and like most tortoises it's a terrestrial type of species.

"Sulcata" is a Latin word which means sculpted or furrowed; if you take a closer look at their shells, legs, and scales you'll notice that they have a lot of furrows and specifications that makes them unique. They have a sandy and ivory shell with huge spurs on their hind legs.

Their top shell or so – called carapace has plates that has a shade of yellow, tan or light brown color that are outlined with brownish colors. Their bottom shell or so – called plastron has the same yellowish and tan color. The skin of the sulcata particularly its legs are covered with spiny and dull projections. The purpose of its spines and hard skin is to protect them against predators in the wild and also functions as insulation keeping them cool during hot days and warm during cold days. Their spurs have no function according to researchers but sometimes they seem to use it if they are happy because they wagged them off like a dog's tail.

The claws of African Spur Thigh is an amazing characteristic because you can't see that in other turtle species since they are water animals and therefore have not developed that kind of physical trait.

Sulcata tortoises live for over 50 years and more! The oldest sulcata tortoise in captivity is around 55 years old (which is housed in a zoo in Egypt), while the oldest recorded tortoise in the wild is around 80 years old. You might be wondering why these creatures can survive that long even if they are in the wild, well that's because they are pure herbivores! They like to nibble grass, cactus or any greens they can find; they can also eat a whole plant!

These factors are beneficial in the ecosystem that they are in while living in the wild because since they eat lots of plants, they also tend to defecate a lot of it which is beneficial because their manure has moisture where the seeds can germinate and their poop can serve as a fertilizer and in a way make them literally create a garden around the burrow that they dug.

When it comes to feeding in captivity, sulcata tortoises are grassland species similar to other species like the Russian, and Greek tortoises as well as the leopard tortoise. These animals are constantly moving around their environment while nibbling on grass. However, grass and weeds don't have nutritional value that's why they're constantly taking it in if they live in the wild. Since you will be feeding them with produce that contains lots of nutrients when they're in captivity, you don't want to over-feed them.

Quick Facts

Taxonomy: Kingdom Animalia, Phylum Chordata, Class Sauropsida, Order Testudines, Family Testudinidae, Genus Centrochelys, Species Sulcata

Distribution and Range: Sahara Desert Africa (specifically in Sahel), Nigeria, Ethiopia, Burkina Faso, Chad, Mali, Mauritania, Sudan, Senegal

Breed Size: 3rd largest tortoise in the world; can grow up to 150 – 200 pounds

Body Type and Appearance: Has furrowed legs and head, has large claws, dull yet thick skin, spiny looking legs and a very sculpted – looking shell

Length: Sulcata Tortoises can grow of up to 33 inches and can reach over 10 inches just within a few years

Weight: They weigh an average of 200 – 250 pounds

Skin Texture: scaly and has a hard sculpted looking shell; its legs are also covered with spiny and dull looking projection

Color: Their top shell has plates that have a shade of yellow, tan or light brown color which are also outlined with brownish colors. Their bottom shell has the same yellowish and tan color.

Temperament: inquisitive, fun, docile, smart, easy to handle and tame, could potentially be aggressive if captured directly in the wild.

Diet: Pure herbivores; they mostly eat plants, grass, flowers, weeds and other green veggies both in the wild and in captivity.

Habitat: Savannahs, Woodlands, Shrublands, Rainforests, and Grasslands

Health Conditions: generally healthy but predisposed to common illnesses such as tortoise prolapse, eye syndrome, lung infection, shell rot and intestinal parasites

Lifespan: average 50 to 80 years

Chapter Two: Sulcata Tortoises as Pets

The main difference between a tortoise and a turtle is that the former are terrestrial type of creatures while the latter are mostly semi – aquatic animals. Compared to turtles, tortoises tend to get much bigger, heavier and most species live longer than turtles. Tortoises and turtles alike are believed to be one of the oldest animal species on earth. Their ancestors go as far back around the time of the dinosaurs and some researchers also believe that they are perhaps the longest living species that survived to this day without evolving much and doesn't have any significant change in terms of their physical characteristics.

In this chapter, you'll learn more about how to deal with them as pets, the costs in keeping them as well as some conservation concerns for its kind.

Reminders Before Getting a Sulcata Tortoise

Before getting yourself into a situation which may later surprise or worse alarm you, you should keep in mind the practicality of owning more than one of these adorable African sulcata tortoises. Below are some reminders:

- Keep in mind that these tiny and adorable creatures will grow fast and will require you a lot of your attention and time. Not only will you have to consider the size it can grow to (which is a whopping 150 pound tortoise that will require some heavy lifting), you will also need to factor in the available space you have at home which may later be swamped with tanks and aquariums if you are not thoughtful.

- As mentioned earlier, sulcata tortoises that are well taken care of in captivity can be expected to live for well over 50 to 80 years. Make sure that you are ready for some very long term commitment because these pets can probably outlive you.

- Keep in mind that it is also illegal to release a tortoise back in the wild. If an individual is caught, one could be heavily fined, so if you become overwhelmed by the baby sulcata tortoises that you bought or produced, you will have to do what is right by researching and looking for ways to correctly disperse them, and not just throw them away.

- Think about how many you can handle up to the time that they grow bigger and older before buying a lot of these pets.

Behavioral Characteristics in the Wild and in Captivity

African sulcata tortoises are the gentlest pets a keeper can ever have, much more so than a very friendly dog or cat! They are perhaps one of the least threatening animals in the world both in captivity and in the wild – I personally think "attack" is not in their vocabulary, and this is mostly because of their – you guessed it - slow pace movement! As we all know they just hide inside their tough hard shells or probably use their thick skinned scaly spurs every now and then to aid them whenever they would feel as if they are being threatened by predators in the wild which is perhaps the best defensive strategy. They literally carry their own shelter wherever they go which makes them live longer and feel secure even if they don't possess any significant striking or offensive skills compared to other reptiles or animals.

They are very hardy tortoises which is part of the reason why they are so popular. These cute little bunches are very active, they start eating right away, and they also possess an amazing shell compared to other tortoises or turtles.

In the wild and even in captivity, sulcata tortoises love to hide and dig large burrows just to get away from the extreme heat of the sun especially for those tortoises living in dryer areas and harsh environments such as in the Sahara desert, rainforests, and woodlands where most sulcata tortoises can be found. Sulcata tortoises also possess some huge claws in their legs which makes them very important creatures in the desert environment that they lived in because since they're the ones who can dig deep holes, other animals tend to share in that shading if they can't come out because it's too hot. Other desert animals like snakes, monitor lizards, iguanas and other reptiles help one another in a way and even live in the bottom part of the burrows that's about 60 feet deep. Most tortoises spend both cold and hot days under these burrows.

African Spur Thigh tortoises are semi – desert to desert species because they are the kind of pets that likes dry environments, but that doesn't mean that you won't provide them water or a cooling area. You will learn more about how to set up an enclosure for your tortoises in the next few chapters. Since they are naturally adapted to a hotter temperature, they have found a way on how to survive despite the harsh conditions by only coming out if the temperature in the desert is just right which is usually around the dawn and dusk hours.

Nocturnal animals are those that are active at night while diurnal animals are those that are active during the day, but sulcata tortoises fall under the category of corpuscular which are species that are neither nocturnal or diurnal because most of the time they're just staying under the burrow that they dug up using their huge claws waiting for the right time and perfect temperature to come out and explore the outside world.

Interaction with other Species

Sulcata tortoises are even-tempered reptiles that could share space with its kind and a few other turtle or younger tortoise species given that they are provided enough room to be housed comfortably. Many hobbyists aim to integrate many of their reptile pets in one habitat and though this is possible and often successfully accomplished by experienced keepers, tanks housing mixed-species of turtles or reptiles can be very challenging to keep clean, is quite costly and can also be time consuming.

Although sulcata tortoises are very friendly and seem non – threatening to humans, they can show aggressiveness towards other tortoise species especially when its territory is threatened or if food is not enough within the enclosure because it can obviously create a competition. It can possibly show its innate rage and prey upon other species if it is housed with other tortoises but as long as you provide them with more than enough space as they grow and give them a fair amount of food and other necessities to live a comfortable captive life, then you won't have a problem with housing them in one habitat.

If you are planning to house multiple species or sulcata tortoises in one tank you will need to follow a thought out strategy to help them be comfortable with one another. You may need to provide a lot of extra space with many hiding places and visible barriers; you also have to ensure that all species are fed separately to make sure that each one is properly fed. No socialization or interaction is needed prior to mixing them with other tortoise species because they can pretty much get along, however if you may need to quarantine new species to prevent the spread of possible illnesses.

Pros and Cons

Pros

- Docile, quiet and non – threatening creatures even if it is not trained or socialized
- Requires no supervision, provided that its enclosure is safe and secured
- Keeping them is not that costly and not hard to maintain during its early years
- Suited for expert keepers and beginners alike
- Mostly available in local pet shops or reptile conventions
- Very easy to feed; they are vegetarian and commercial foods are also available in reptile shops or major pet stores
- Unlikely to get ill with appropriate care
- Doesn't shed and doesn't need to be groomed
- Very fun to keep and easy to raise especially when they're still hatchlings or juveniles

Cons

- Growth may be relatively hard to manage since they can get huge and heavier over time.
- Costs for food, caging and other materials when they reach adulthood could become relatively expensive.
- May not be an ideal pet if you only live in a small house because it needs lots of space as it grows; this pet is ideal for keepers who have a backyard
- They may need supervision once it reaches adulthood
- Keeping more than one tortoise can be harder to maintain in the long run and also time consuming
- If you become a breeder of these species, you need to make sure that you can take care of all the hatchlings as they grow up because it's hard to find rescue centers, put them up for adoption or even give them to people if you won't be able to handle their needs one day.
- Can live up to 50 years or more which means that long – term commitment is needed.

Tortoise Legalities

There are varying degrees in which legal protection is afforded to sulcata tortoises but due to continuous illegal capture in certain areas it can still be a threat to this species.

You won't really need to get a license if you decide to keep or breed these adorable creatures because they are listed in the Appendix II of the Convention on International Trade in Endangered Species (CITES) which means that they can be traded for commercial purposes but they can't be taken from the wild unless you got the approval of wildlife organizations or authorities. Since tortoises like the sulcata falls under the Appendix II category it also implies that you will not be allowed to transport these tortoises from one country to another if you don't have an export certificate from wildlife organizations and from your country of origin. You'll also need to secure an import certificate to the country of your destination.

If you want to travel or transport your pet tortoise, you should have these certificates in order to satisfy authorities that your pet is obtained legally. It may vary from one state/country to another but authorities may need to check document that states the name and identity of your sulcata tortoises. You'll also need to state your name address, contact details as well as other personal information to be kept for future reference and also for legality purposes. If as a keeper or breeder you don't comply with the regulations of CITES, authorities has grounds to automatically confiscate your pet tortoises, pay a fine, and even face (bailable) imprisonment. If you're going to buy or sell sulcata tortoises from other countries, you'll need an authorization for import to make sure that they will be legally imported.

Tortoises being traded in other countries sometimes can be hard for authorities to differentiate whether or not they are wild or captive – bred specimens which sometimes contribute to illegal importation.

Threats to Conservation

Smuggling of these tortoises particularly in African countries like Ghana, Senegal, Togo and Mali are evident because enforcement is insufficient which is why wildlife advocates are aiming to address this problem. The good thing is that these African sulcata tortoises thrives in captivity and breeds easily in countries like United States and Japan making it enough to supply the demand for these pets.

In Senegal, these tortoises are more than just pets, they are symbols of longevity, happiness and fertility which is why conservation activities are much easier to promote and maintain compared to other African regions. In fact, in 1993, a European foundation called Fondation Rurale pour le Developpement in partnership with Station d'Observation et de Protection des Tortues des Maures established a program to educate the people of Senegal on how to protect illegal smuggling of pet tortoises. They've also established an information, breeding and protection center and even initiated some conservation projects to further protect these species, which is why despite of the continuous desertification threat in the country, there are still a lot of people who are willing to preserve these wildlife gems.

In other African countries (such as Ethiopia, Nigeria, Mali and Chad) where sulcata tortoises are native and previously abundant are increasingly declining in terms of population because of natural habitat loss due to domestic livestock and continuous urbanization. Aside from that, African nomads and ethnic groups that are residing in the Sahara desert also contribute to this decrease in population because they are eating these creatures and some groups even use the tortoise's body parts. In Japan, sulcatas are reportedly being used to create longevity potions!

It will take about 15 years before African spurred thigh tortoise reaches full maturity in the wild, which is why juvenile sulcatas are the ones targeted for illegal trades. This raises a huge concern among wildlife experts and legit breeders in its native African origins because these creatures could face the possibility of extinction.

Costs of Keeping a Pet Tortoise

The sultaca tortoise is a relatively affordable pet, hence its wide popularity. The upside of getting an African sulcata is that it can easily be obtained for as low as $20 in a pet store. If you choose to acquire it from legit reptile breeders, you can expect a price ranging from $50 to $80 depending on the breeder as well as the age of the tortoise.

Again, you should consider the availability of space in your home as these tortoises can grow to be quite big as it matures. If you want to buy it for a more affordable price, you may opt to search online if there's any sulcata tortoise in your area being given up for adoption. There are also non-profit and rescue organizations you should visit because rescuing one can be really beneficial to the environment and you can acquire them for a relatively cheaper price or even for free!

At the onset, it could cost you about $125 or more for its housing needs – that usually includes a 10 – 20 gallon tank or a DIY tortoise table complete with other caging materials for decorations and water bowl. The heaters, UVB lights, basking platforms, hideouts, substrate and other additional fixtures needed could cost more or less $300.

You'll probably spend around $40 per week for 30 pounds of vegetables and fruit unless of course you choose to just feed them with grass or weeds found in your backyard. They can live with that but as a keeper, it's probably best to provide them with food that has the right nutrients so that they can grow healthily.

Don't forget to factor in the expense for cage maintenance to remove dirt and bacteria (especially in their water bowls). Tortoises pretty much poop a lot (that's basically because they are herbivores – they tend to digest and defecate food easily) which means that their tank or enclosure should ideally be cleaned at least every other day to avoid the incidence of parasites, infections and shell rot. You will also want to factor in the yearly electricity costs of keeping a terrarium clean, tempered, lit and conditioned to the needs of the sulcata tortoise.

You also need to buy a laying bin if in case you'd be breeding your sulcata tortoises. You can either buy some kind of reptile container or a standard laying bin in pet stores. The breeding cost will vary depending on the quality, so you should budget about $50 or more for these extra costs.

Sulcata tortoises will need minimal medical attention but it is strongly suggested that you take your baby sulcatas to the vet after acquiring them to make sure that they are healthy before bringing them home and mixing them with your other tortoise or turtle species. You'll pretty much need to bring your tortoise to the vet for a quick check up if you choose to breed them as well. But generally speaking, you won't have to worry about huge medical costs or even a pet insurance for these animals – remember, they live very long and healthy lives, there's an even bigger chance of you acquiring an illness than them.

Tortoises must be treated in a way that an expensive pure bred puppy would be treated not because they are hard to maintain but because they can still make quite a dent to your bank account, nevertheless they are fun and adorable lifelong friends which makes them worth your time and money.

Breakdown of Costs:

- **Sulcata Tortoise species**: $20 - $80 or more
- **10 to 20 gallon tank/ tortoise table + caging materials** (wood, glass terrarium, plants, water dishes, cage decorations, cleaning materials): more or less $125 (depends on the cage quality)
- **Bedding or Substrate:** $6/bag
- **Heaters/Heat Pads:** around $40
- **Basking Lamp/UVB bulbs:** $30 or more
- **Hiding Spots:** $5 - $10 for hatchlings/juveniles
- **Food:** average of $40 per week for 30 pound bag (prices can vary depending on brand and amount/quantity)
- **Laying bin + additional breeding materials:** $50
- **Total Cost:** more or less $300

Chapter Three: Acquiring Sulcata Tortoises

It's essential that before you purchase any kinds of reptile for this matter, you should first consider on who bred and raised them. Keep in mind that purchasing a healthy breed is one of the most essential things that every potential reptile keeper should learn about. In this chapter you will be provided with the criteria on selecting a healthy sulcata tortoise and be given criteria to spot a reputable and trustworthy breeder. You will also learn where to legally purchase tortoises. You'll also be provided with links to possibly legit breeders and rescue centers.

Rescue Centers vs. Legit Breeders vs. Pet Stores

Before comparing the benefits of adopting tortoises from rescue centers and purchasing from hobbyists or legit breeders, it's probably best to first address why buying from pet stores is somewhat discouraged. We all know that pet shops are the go – to place when it comes to purchasing different kinds of animals like sulcata tortoises but the main downside in buying from such pet stores especially those that are not locally recognized shops is that there's a nine of ten instances that these local pet shops don't really care about the pets that they sell.

Based from many experienced keepers, these pet shops are only selling pets for the money. Of course, it's still a business but the thing is that you can't be assured of the pet's health. I'm not saying that all local pet shops are selling unhealthy breeds but most of the time they don't really care for this pets which should be your top most concerned as a potential keeper. You would want to acquire a species that is a product of good breeding practices to ensure that they are not sick or doesn't carry other diseases which could affect your collection (if you have one) and to also ensure that they are not illegally obtained. Pet stores housing sulcata tortoises with other exotic animals from other countries is also to be avoided as these exotic animals could be carriers of diseases which could be passed on to the tortoise.

Bottom line is that, as much as possible, acquire a pet tortoise from rescue centers, from legit breeders or even hobbyists found in reptile conventions because it eliminates lots of risks in terms of breeding and husbandry in the long run since legit breeders are passionate about raising such animals.

In terms of adopting adult and even hatchling sulcata tortoises, you can have a hard time finding them because there are some rescue centers that doesn't cater to tortoises or other reptile species since these creatures gets bigger; these centers obviously cannot provide enough housing space.

There could be pet shelters and a rescue center that accommodates sulcata tortoises but that depends on your location. The reasons why these adorable creatures end up in rescues is because they could have escaped its confines or most of the time an overwhelmed hobbyist may have bitten off more than what he/she could chew and couldn't take care of the pet properly. Adopting from rescues is not only a good way to give the tortoise a new loving keeper, but it also discourages the purchase of hatchlings from indiscriminate tortoise breeders who are only out to make a quick buck.

The best part is that if you have found a healthy and sweet looking sulcata from one of these rescue centers, they could be much cheaper to buy compared to acquiring one from a hobbyist or a legit breeder.

With that being said about rescue centers, it's best that you also consider acquiring one from a hobbyist either directly or through pet conventions so that you can have more options. The great thing about hobbyists is that you can ask them questions about how they raise these tortoises, the requirements and specifications they would need as well as why they're doing it. You can easily see why it's better to buy one from them than from a pet store because these breeders are passionate about their pets and very knowledgeable about them; after all they're the ones who raised them. However, you should also look out for private breeders that are just looking to make cash out of these creatures because they could be breeding for breeding's sake.

You don't want to get a tortoise that are pre – matured or somewhat sick looking due to bad breeding practices or poor husbandry. Be wary of such breeders, who are claiming to be hobbyists, because there are a lot of them out there. They could have smuggled pets from foreign sources or must have picked them out from the wild which is illegal based on several wildlife organizations.

When it comes to purchasing pet tortoises, always buy it from a breeder that is reputable, trustworthy, truly passionate and also a professional. In the next section, you'll learn the qualities to look out for on a breeder and the characteristics of a healthy sulcata tortoise.

Selecting a Reputable Breeder and a Healthy Tortoise

It is quite challenging to identify a reputable reptile breeder from "fake" breeders. These are common when tortoises are bred in captivity. Most breeders today breed African spurred thighs because it's an increasingly popular household pet. So it will still be largely up to you to research and seek out the best breeders who are open to answering questions about the origins of the tortoise, the methods employed during production and hatch period as well as other important husbandry practices he/she have done.

If a breeder lets you walk - through in their facilities to see the conditions and living environment of the animals housed within their site, that's a great indicator of a legit breeder; all these could indicate a breeder who aims to follow the protocol for breeding these tortoises. Stay away from super discounted sulcata tortoise traders since the discount itself could be a giveaway of an abundance of pets resulting to slashed prices in order to get rid of excess hatchlings. After determining your reputable breeder, and assessing your financial capabilities, you will have to conduct a very simple physical exam to ensure that the species you will get is worth the investment.

Sulcata tortoises should be alert, active and inquisitive. They should not appear lethargic and if you give them food, they should at least have an appetite for it. Pick up the turtle and determine whether it weighs heavy or light because a light turtle may be ill. The next test is to gently tug at one of its legs. The reaction of an ill turtle will be slow and less vigorous whereas a healthy turtle will be quick to react strongly. You should also scrutinize the top and bottom halves of its shell. They should be sandy or smooth, hard and has yellowish or light brown shaded plates with furrowed but spiny looking legs. If the shell is soft once you touch it, this could indicate shell rot. Take note of the occurrence of open wounds, discharge from eyes and their interaction with other pets.

List of Breeders and Rescue Websites

Going to a reptile pet shop or rescue center is convenient but going online to buy your sulcata tortoise will save you some money. If you want to see your chosen tortoise up close and personal, however, you may want to opt for local breeders in your area, speak to other sulcata breeders or try looking for reptile online groups. The people in these groups are usually knowledgeable about reptiles and tortoises in general, and may give you good advice on where to acquire an African Spurred Thigh.

List of Breeders and Rescue Websites

Tortoise Town

<https://www.tortoisetown.com/>

Tortoise Yard

<https://tortoiseyard.com/>

Kingsnake

<http://market.kingsnake.com/index.php?cat=50>

Back Water Reptiles

<http://www.backwaterreptiles.com/tortoises/sulcata-tortoise-for-sale.html>

Arizona Sulcata

<http://azsulcata.com/>

Tortoise Supply

<http://www.tortoisesupply.com/>

Tortoise Home Farm

<http://tortoisehomefarm.org/leopard-sulcata-tortoise-for-sale/>

The Turtle Source

<http://www.theturtlesource.com/i.asp?id=225689789>

Underground Reptiles

<https://undergroundreptiles.com/shop/baby-sulcata-tortoise/>

Ivory Tortoise

<http://ivorytortoise.com/buy_a_tortoise/african_spurred.php>

South Florida Rodents

<https://southfloridarodents.com/tag/baby-sulcata-tortoise-for-sale/>

Adopt – A – Pet

<http://www.adoptapet.com/s/tortoise-adoption>

North Tortoise

<http://northwesttortoise.org/at-turtletopia/rescue-and-adoptions-2/>

SD Turtle

<https://www.sdturtle.org/adoptions>

Chapter Four: Suitable Environment for Sulcata Tortoises

Part of keeping a pet tortoise is ensuring that they are well – housed in an environment that feels like their natural habitat in the wild. You have to prepare an ample space in your house where they can roam around as they get older and set up a terrarium with all the basic necessities they need in order to grow happy and healthy.

In this chapter, you'll learn the housing requirements suited for baby or juvenile sulcatas or African spurred thighs tortoises. We'll discuss on the basic things they need and you'll also learn the reason why these factors can contribute to making your pet feel safe and comfortable.

Housing Requirements for Baby Tortoises

You have to compare your baby sulcata tortoise with a real life baby. They're like little toddlers walking around and investigating things, they're curious and they basically wanted to learn how to get along with other species and deal with life. With that being said you have to ensure that the habitat you set up will provide their environmental needs and is not dangerous for them. If you have a collection of other sulcata tortoises, there'll be times that you see them flipping over lying in the back of their shells just like toddlers, so you have to also ensure that all the ornaments or cage decorations you place inside the enclosure are easy enough for them to get in and out of.

Enclosure Options for Sulcata Tortoises

When it comes to housing a sulcata tortoise, you have to keep in mind that they like to be in a solid structure where they can't see through. Compared to turtles, tortoises will totally spend their time pacing the glass so it's important that you put them in an enclosure or tank where they cannot see through. If you want other people to easily view your pet or if you're going to buy a glass terrarium, it's probably better if you black out the rest of the enclosure's sides and only leave one clear side of the glass.

This is the reason why a wooden tortoise table is ideal especially for land dwellers like the sulcata tortoises, you can search online for tortoise table ideas and you can even buy and assemble a wooden enclosure from pet stores. If you're sort of a craftsman, why not form your own tortoise table and design a do – it – yourself terrarium? This can somewhat save you a few bucks and you can create it in a specification of your choice.

Another option is to turn old wooden bookshelves (if you happen to have one at home). Just clean them up, turn them on the side and make sure that the bottom part is strong and intact because that's obviously where you will put all the substrate and cage materials for your tortoise. Ensure that it doesn't fall off or have any holes where your baby tortoises can sneak through. If you do that you can easily save money and time rather than building one yourself.

If you don't prefer wooden enclosures, but still want to save money or you don't have the time to shop for terrariums, you can easily purchase a cheap wide plastic tub or mixing tubs (preferably not the clear ones) from your local home depot. These tubs can be a perfect alternative for glass terrariums because they are open. This is the major advantage of these open tubs because you can easily lift it up, its light since it's made out of plastic and you can easily place it outside your house so that your baby tortoises can get some natural sunlight, though you may need to put a screen to keep them safe from birds or other predators. Make sure to also remove it if the weather becomes bad outside. Tubs are suitable nursing enclosures for hatchlings at least for the next 6 months.

Basking Materials

Basking your sulcata tortoise is very important for the development of its shell so make sure that you provide them with the lights and heat they need for them to have basking options within their enclosure. You can choose from different kinds of basking light since there are lots of products out there that provide bright lights which could help your tortoise and fit inside your enclosure.

There are different types of heating equipment including a ceramic heater which could provide a lot more heat and could easily heat up a larger space or big enclosures; another one is called halogen bulbs which are good to develop your pet's shell. You can also purchase a rheostat because it can also aid in regulating lighting temperature inside the enclosure.

One of the basking options is called a ceramic heater this kind of heating equipment will obviously not give off any light because it only provides nothing but pure heat, this may not be suitable if your enclosure is a Rubbermaid tub. It works best for tanks or glass terrariums. Ceramic heaters are lasts for a long time and can be beneficial because sulcatas prefers a humid surrounding.

The next option for basking is halogen bulbs; this kind of equipment is could be very hot and very bright for your pet tortoise. This is also suitable for baby sulcata tortoises because it's safer.

If you purchase a low wattage bulb, you can just have two or three of it, and put it over a section of the cage providing your pet with a basking zone. The downside is that halogen bulbs tend to break easily if it is moved too much. However, buying two or three of these halogen bulbs is better than just purchasing one thick bulb; this is because a thick bulb can create a hot spot or even burn your pet whereas the three bulb spread across a portion of the enclosure is much more ideal in providing the needed temperature in the basking area.

Your pet will also need UVB bulb. It's very important equipment for basking especially if you won't have the time to expose them under the sun every morning. These bulbs will simulate the sun's heat.

After purchasing those lights and heating equipment, you can have two options when it comes to its set up. The first is that you can choose to buy a lighting bulb and UVB bulb and attached it to a fixture located on one side of the enclosure so that your pet can have an area where they can bask in. The second option is for you to buy a single lamp that will provide lighting through the entire enclosure then attached the same UVB bulb in your fixture and place it on one side so that your pet tortoise can have both options available – the light and the heat.

Substrate

You should opt to purchase reptibar type of substrate because it can stay dry and can also be moist if you have other pet turtles that are semi – aquatic. You can also take organic potting soil and mix it together to create a substrate. Reptibar substrate is not something that your sulcata tortoise will nibble on so you don't have to worry about impaction, just make sure that you don't mist it since most tortoises likes dryer surface. It's also easy to spot clean because you can easily scoop your pet's poop; it's also very neat looking.

Water Dish

The first thing a baby tortoise need is water. It doesn't matter if a tortoise is from a desert or a jungle; you have to make sure that you provide with clean water for your young sulcata tortoises. It's highly recommended that you purchase shallow water bowls because if you buy water dishes that are deep or big enough for their size, they can accidentally flip over and if you don't notice them they can definitely die since they're not aquatic species like turtles. Don't fill up the water bowl too deep, just place an amount where they can easily put their heads under to drink and a dish that they can get out of if in case they flip on their backs to avoid drowning.

Food Dish

You can buy different kinds of food dish that comes in many sizes and colors from pet stores or you can save money by purchasing a flower pot dish made out of clay. You can easily get it at hardware stores or local home centers for a very cheap price. You have to keep in mind that, just like the water dish, the food dish/bowl is also shallow where your baby tortoise can conveniently access. The advantage of using a clay or rough type of food dish is that it could develop your tortoise beak or mouth because as it eats in the dish, it can naturally scratch off its excess beak. If you use plastic or stainless food dishes, it can cause problems because they are not being fed on something hard which can cause problems since their beak will become too long or overgrown. If this happens you might need to use some trimming device to cut off the excess beak which can be quite an unpleasant experience for your baby sulcatas.

Misting and Soaking

Just do a light misting once or twice a day to replicate dew in the morning or the moist they experience in their natural surroundings. Even if sulcata tortoises are from deserts, it's important that they stay hydrated.

Small Plastic Enclosure for Soaking

This is optional if you want to soak your sulcata tortoise, you can do these at thrice a week especially if you live in a warmer location. Just fill it up with a bit of water and let them soak there for about 10 minutes. If you want to know if you're tortoise is sufficiently hydrated, once you soak it sometimes they will expel a white toothpaste gooey looking substance on their rear end, don't be worried because that's actually an indicator that they are hydrated. If you see this white stuff in a more powder form, you may need to soak them more and keep them really hydrated because that means that they are holding off moisture inside of its body, this is their survival tactic in the wild if they cannot find water in the desert, now since you took on the responsibility of keeping them, it's now your job to make sure that they are well – hydrated and not be stressed out in their environment.

Hiding Areas with Sphagnum Moss

If tortoises are not provided with a humid hiding area it tends to make their shells go much rougher. What you can do is to provide a humid hiding spot where they can bask or burrow. You should provide them with spag moss (something that you can buy in a pet store or something that is placed for indoor plants). What you should do is to soak the spag moss in some water, squeeze out the excess water, and place it underneath the hiding area or cave. This will provide a humid area that your tortoise can enjoy. When it comes to purchasing a hiding area, you can choose from several designs found in pet shops, just make sure to adjust the size as your tortoise gets bigger over time. If you're in a tight budget, what you can do is to get a boot of a tree or some sort of log where your sulcata turtles can go under, don't forget to put the moist spag moss inside so that you can make a realistic replica of their natural environment. Just put it all there and allow the animal to seek it out within the enclosure, they will pretty much use it to bask or nestle in which is perfect for their overall shell covering.

Chapter Five: Feeding and Nutrition

Feeding your tortoise is not that hard, in fact, you won't have to worry about it at all. If you happen to have a backyard outside or some plants, your sulcata can live a happy life! But since you took on the responsibility of becoming a reputable keeper or breeder, it's probably best that you live up to that by providing them with a healthy nutrition. Fresh produce, hay, commercial pellets and occasional fruity treats as well as their natural food in the wild like grass, flowers and weeds can all contribute in the longevity and health of your pet. In this chapter, you'll learn the nutritional value your pet needs and some tips on how to serve it to them. You'll also find a list of toxic plants that you should avoid offering.

Nutritional Requirements

The key to a tortoise's long life is proper diet. The diet of tortoises in general should be high in fiber and calcium yet low in protein and fruit; the kind of food a keeper should feed depends on the type of tortoise. In this case, sulcata tortoises should be fed with hay since it is high in fiber and highly recommended for grassland tortoises like the African spurred thighs and other species that originated from arid landscapes.

There are basically two types of hay; timothy hay and alfafa hay. Alfafa hay contains high levels of fiber and calcium but it also contain higher levels of protein than timothy hay, so make sure that you don't overfeed your pet sulcata with too much alfafa hay. Hay can be purchased per bag and are often found in pet shops, groceries and through online retailers. If you don't see hay in the reptile section, you can find stocks in probably the rabbit or guinea pig sections.

Other foods for grassland tortoises include grass, flowers, and weeds. Keep in mind that in the wild, tortoises graze on the ground which is why grass should also be available. If you don't have plenty of grass around your backyard, you can easily purchase grass seeds so that you can grow your own grass so that your pet sulcata can graze happily outside. If you keep your pet in an outdoor pen, what you can do is plant edible grasses and other plants so that they can have plenty of options.

If you plan to let your pet sulcata graze or if you're picking wild grasses, weeds or other type of vegetation for them to eat, just make sure to offer them fresh produce that are not sprayed with pesticides. It's also important to know which plants are toxic so that you don't accidentally give anything poisonous to your tortoise. Below is the list of toxic plants for your sulcata tortoise:

List of Toxic Plants to Avoid

Here's a list of plants that could be harmful for your pet sulcata tortoise:

- Aconite
- Anemone
- Azalea
- Begonia
- Bird of Paradise
- Buttercup
- Calla Lily
- Cyclamen
- Daffodil
- Dianthus
- Foxglove
- Hemlock
- Hydrangea
- Ivy
- Lily of the Valley
- Lobelia
- Mistletoe
- Nightshade
- Oleander
- Prunus
- Ragwort
- Rhododendron
- Sweet Pea

Go Green!

Plants like collard greens, mustard greens and dandelion greens are all nutritious and packed with high levels of calcium. You can easily purchase collard and mustard greens in grocery stores, dandelion greens on the other hand can be a bit hard to find but you can always have the option to grow your own.

Sulcata tortoises love to eat Dandelion flowers as well as Hibiscus, Rose petals and carnation. You can offer them other types of flowers but make sure that they are non - toxic and are not sprayed with fertilizers or pesticides. It could be tempting to buy lots of fresh veggies in supermarkets but you need to keep in mind that these veggies may not be good choices because greens like spinach because it can block the tortoise's ability to absorb calcium.

Some vegetables like peas and green beans contain high levels of protein, Iceberg lettuces should also be avoided because it can cause diarrhea to tortoises since it has high water content. Fruit can be offered as a treat but make sure that you don't overfeed your pet with it or offer fruits that have high water content. Fruits like strawberries, blueberries, raspberry, cantelope, apple, papaya and mango are good fruits to feed as long as you offer it to them in limited amounts.

Before you offer fresh foods to your sulcatas, it's highly recommended that you sprinkled it with a small amount of calcium supplement preferably with Vitamin D3 and without any phosphorous content for each serving.

Commercial Foods

Commercial pellets can also be rotated as part of your pet's diet. You can purchase them through pet stores or online. Just make sure that before you buy one, you check out the list of ingredients contain in each pack. Plan your pet's nutrition accordingly and look forward to spending a long term relationship with your tortoise.

Chapter Six: Husbandry for Sulcata Tortoise

This chapter will delve deeper on how to house and take care of adult sulcata tortoises. Once they become fully mature and have reached over 100 pounds or more, obviously you won't be able to contain them in their previous enclosures. If you don't have a big backyard or you only have a limited space, you can still house them comfortably by creating a play pen where they can be free to roam around outside your house yet preventing them from getting away. You'll learn how to build a pen and the ideal location of your growing tortoises. You'll also get some tips on how to protect them against predators so that they will be safe walking outside.

Building a Tortoise Pen for Adult Sulcatas

As you now know, sulcata tortoises are better off living outside since these creatures are originally land dwellers or grassland species. Once they become huge, the best habitat for them is outdoors so that they can also get direct heat from the sun to make them healthy. Artificial UVB bulbs or lights may not be sufficient for them anymore, ultraviolet rays from the sun is now a necessity because it will aid in the production of Vitamin D3 which will help your tortoise absorb the calcium that they need to keep their body and shell healthy.

If your sulcata tortoise becomes too large for your house inside, it's time to relocate them by creating a tortoise or turtle pen. The bigger the pen, the better for your tortoise, this is because it will replicate their habitat in the wild which is much ideal for them.

Ideal Size of the Pen

When building a play pen, you also have to make sure that they are not overcrowded; this is for owners who are considering of keeping more than one sulcata tortoise or housing them with other tortoise or turtle species. Overcrowding can lead to poor hygiene and even territoriality issues among inhabitants.

The ideal pen size for tortoises in general should be 3 sq. ft. per each inch of its shell. Juvenile or growing sulcatas can be housed in a pen that's about 4 x 3 feet in size; adult tortoises should be double or triple than the recommended size.

How to Build a Play Pen

Building a play pen for your adult sulcata tortoises is just like designing their enclosure when they were still young and small. You can basically get creative and just let your imagination and taste for aesthetic run wild. There are no specific rules but the guidelines below can give you an idea on how to build one or where to place one if you have a larger space outside.

Ideal Location Tips

- Build your pen in a space where your tortoise can have lots of sunshine
- You can also choose to place it in a sort of slope or elevated soil if you have one so that your tortoise can easily turn itself back up if it gets flipped over. If you
- Place it in a spot where it is safe from any hazard or drainage since it can be prone to flooding

Ideal Temperature

If you are located in a place where the climate has hot summers and relatively cold winters, you can possibly let them stay outdoors all year round because that could be an ideal temperature for your pet sulcata. If that's not the case and the condition may be too harsh for your pet especially at night, you can still let them play outside every morning or at least throughout the day to catch some sunlight and also get some exercise.

If you have enough space outside, you can try building a green house where your tortoise can bask in and stay heated if the temperature outside are too cold for them. You can choose to build something that has a plastic roof on top so that the sun's infrared rays can still pass through and still benefit your tortoise.

The basking spot should be around 90 degrees Fahrenheit or a bit higher than that since these creatures prefer warmer temperature just like in the desert. If you built a green house, the sun can still heat up the enclosure at about 18 degrees Fahrenheit warmer than the cooler temperature outside the green house.

Male to Female Tortoise Ratio

Aside from the recommended size of the pen or green house enclosure that you will build outside for your adult tortoise, you also need to think about the ratio of the male and female tortoise if you're going to house them in the same enclosure. If you don't want them to breed or if you only have a limited space outside, you should just stick to keeping female tortoises. This is because female tortoises get along better than their counterparts. If you own a couple of male tortoises, you should also make sure to separate them or as much as possible not housed them in one enclosure as they tend to become aggressive towards other male tortoises.

If you house both male and female tortoises together, make sure that the ratio is 1:4 (one male to 4 females); this is because male tortoises are known to chasing female tortoises constantly, if the female tortoise is always getting chased, she can get stressed out and this could lead to her getting sick. As much as possible, don't house different tortoises or turtles in one enclosure unless you have a really huge backyard where they can have more than enough space to be separated from one another.

How to Protect Tortoises from Predators

The main disadvantage of letting your pet roam around outside is that you won't be able to always supervise them, and while you can eliminate the risks of hazards by placing the pen or green house in a safe location, they could still be at risk because of predators – this will include your other household pets like cats or dogs, smaller pests like ants and real outside predators like raccoons, birds or other wild animals.

One of the biggest threats to tortoises are dogs, there have been many cases where a dog is housetrained and properly socialize to get along with other pets but because of animal instinct for some reason, owners often end up finding that their dog has caused serious injury to their pet tortoises or turtles. Make sure to supervise your dog if you're going to let him mingle with your tortoise and never leave your pet sulcata on its own devises. This is why your tortoise pen should preferably have a fence or a border as well as a rooftop of some sort for added protection against other animals.

Another common threat for tortoises living outside is pests and insects like fire ants, bees and other poisonous creatures. Your tortoise will surely munch on the grass or plants nearby but the problem is that this is also where such harmful insects hang out or lives to prevent this from happening; you can use a bait trap so that these ants will die or use other alternatives. Don't spray pesticides because your tortoise can absorb these chemicals and cause them to get sick.

Chapter Seven: Handling and Bathing Your Sulcata Tortoise

Handling your tortoise while they are still hatchlings or juveniles is a great training for them because it teaches them how to socialize and become tamed when being touched. Although, tortoises and turtles in general are non – threatening animals, they can still become aggressive if they aren't tamed properly. One of the best ways in taming them is through proper handling. In this chapter, you'll learn how to handle your pet sulcata and also give you instructions on how to groom them so that you can maintain their gorgeous shells and health.

Proper Handling of Sulcata Tortoise

You can have your sulcata tortoise get used to you by just carrying them around while they're still young, just keep them around the house or with other same species so that your pet can be socialized. If your pet is socialized, it can make them less shy when being touched or viewed. Some hatchlings will be quite skittish at first which is why you need to also be careful in handling them so that they won't get traumatize by the experience otherwise they could hate being around with people or be wary to being touched.

Picking up a tortoise is fairly easy when they're young, you just simply have to grab the bottom and top art of their shell just right in the center using your fingers so that they won't be able to push you off or slide off.

Once your tortoise is calm and assuming that they're properly socialized, you can let them walk around your palms but don't raise them up too high as they could slip out and fall especially when they get older and stronger. Properly hold their shells and apply a tight grip on the center top and bottom. Never hold the side of the shells because their rear legs can easily push your finger and they could fall off.

When your tortoise gets a bit larger and heavier, you should start holding both sides of the top and bottom shell using your hands to provide support. Sometimes juvenile tortoises will push you off using their feet, so you just need to have a slightly tight grip over them but of course, not to the point of squeezing them too hard.

Make sure to wash your hands after holding your tortoises because they can potentially have salmonella. It's also a good practice to wash your hands before holding them, and try not to touch their face, eyes, mouths or legs too much.

Once your pet sulcata reaches maturity and has become full grown, you obviously won't be able to simply hold them even with your hands; it will totally require some heavy lifting on your part. Just make sure to handle them carefully, try not to put them on their backs and support the shell with both hands. If you think you can't lift them up because they're too heavy, it's probably best to let someone help you so that you won't risk dropping your tortoise and possibly damaging their shell.

Bathing Your Pet Sulcata

Many people are confused when someone tells them to bathe or groom their tortoises, for the most part, it looks like they don't really need a bath since they don't shed, they are used to being dirty since they're constantly walking in the ground, grazing the grass and they can still be considered wild animals – and wild animals don't take a bath!

There's another tortoise misconception out there that if you bought a particular commercial product for your pet's shell it could make it shiny and or could give the shell some sort of nutrients. That's not true and most of the time these products are harmful since they have chemical content.

The carapace (top shell) and plastron (bottom shell) of your tortoise is composed of tissues, pores, keratin, and nerves, it requires sunlight and oxygen to keep them healthy so if you apply wax, oils or other commercial products it can accumulate and clog your tortoise's pores which can eventually lead to problems. So if you want to keep your tortoise's shell "shiny" and keep them clean, all they need is a clean water, container, and good old tooth brush. Of course, you may need to adjust the brush as they get bigger.

Young or juvenile sulcata tortoises are quite easy to clean because you can still handle them, but once they reach their full size, you may need to rethink how you're going to clean them up or decide on how you're going to house them. Usually you just need to provide a small water lagoon in your yard or garden where your tortoise can easily access and soak in thereby naturally cleaning themselves up.

Bathing a tortoise is not a necessity because they're simply used to getting dirty, but again, since you took on the responsibility of keeping one, it's your job to make sure that they are clean and receive occasionally bathing for health's sake and to also prevent spreading of dirt around the house or its enclosure – the best part is, it's completely safe to do so.

Bathing Materials:

- Container/Tub
- Water (depends on how big your pet is – just make sure it's not filled up too much)
- Toothbrush
- Cotton Buds
- Towel or dry cloth

How to Bathe Your Tortoise

Place your tortoise in the tub and allow it to hydrate himself for about 10 minutes to 20 minutes, after which you can replace the water. Fill the container again with clean water that is no deeper than the tortoise's plastron and just about a few centimeters deep above its top shell.

Once you do, you should again allow your pet to rehydrate and replace their water stores. While your tortoise is doing that, you can now prepare your bathing tools like a toothbrush. Keep in mind that you don't need to put any kind of soap, detergent, oils, shampoo or other cleaning materials that has chemical content. Just a fresh clean water and toothbrush will do. Your main objective here is to just simply clean out the shell and their legs, they're not supposed to smell good or even look good like other household pets.

Once you've prepared your brush, just gently brush their top shell particularly the areas where dirt can often build up as well as the sides. Make sure to clean their scutes and you can also slightly clean their head, legs, neck and tail using cotton buds. When brushing their body parts that are not covered with scales or shells, make sure to gently rub it because these areas could be sensitive. Clean up their claws thoroughly since this is one of the dirtiest parts of your tortoise's body.

After cleaning the top and side of the shells, you can gently flip them over to clean the bottom shell or the plastron. Pay attention to the dirt between their scutes and rub it carefully.

Once you're done removing the dirt, you can now rinse them with water. Don't use any unnecessary product (unless recommended by your vet) because it can be fatal for some tortoise. These products can mix with water and your tortoise can ingest it.

Tortoises don't really shed skin but sometimes you can see their paper thin scutes peeling off like fragments, it's quite normal and you can aid in removing that whenever you are brushing them up because it can allow for a much healthier shell.

After you have rinsed them off, take them out of the water, and dry them up using a soft towel or cloth. Gently do this at least once or twice a week or even once a month (it's entirely up to you) so that your tortoise can be nice and clean.

If you are properly following the husbandry tips and feeding your pet with a healthy diet, their shell will naturally shine by itself without the need for any product. The main advantage of bathing your tortoise is that, it gives an opportunity for owners to thoroughly examine or check their pet if there'll be any sign of illness, shell rot, injury or even abrasion.

Occasional cleaning will make your tortoise feel neat, happy and healthy. This procedure will also maintain their skin and avoid the rotting of their shells.

Chapter Eight: Breeding and Shipping Sulcata Tortoises

African Sulcata tortoises can usually mate the entire year but their breeding season happens during autumn when the temperature in the morning is a bit cooler. In the wild and even in captivity, males court females by directly chasing them and getting in front of them. They will not stop until a female tortoise completely stops so that the male can mount her and start mating. When they these animals copulate, you can expect grunts and loud noises.

If you house a female with a male tortoise and the space is not large enough, males can sometimes damage the female by aggressively chasing her or like what was mentioned in the previous chapter, the female can get stressed out. You may want to always check flipped tortoises especially during the breeding season. In this chapter you'll learn more about how they copulate and how many eggs they usually lay.

Sexual Dimorphism

Sulcata tortoises are sexually dimorphic which means that you can easily identify which one is male or female based on their physical characteristics. Although both sexes look identical, males have concave bottom shells with thicker and longer tales. Their rectal openings are also quite wide than females. They are also larger and have a more prominent gular On the other hand, females are relatively smaller than male sulcatas and their anal scutes in their plastron has a much smaller opening than that of the males.

Nesting

Nesting usually happens around 6 to 8 weeks after copulation, you'll know this when you see your female sulcata digging holes using its front legs. They usually burrow against a wall or near a tree/plant. Once they complete their digging process, the female excavates their egg chamber and starts laying eggs. They usually cover their nest in a meticulous way and the whole nesting process can take hours (since tortoises/turtles are slow creatures).

Compared to other tortoises, sulcatas takes a long time to cover their nest, sometimes it could take them 2 to 3 days just to make sure that the eggs are fully covered. During this time, some female sulcatas can also become overly aggressive if they found out that people or other species are near their nests.

Be careful if you're going to aid in their nesting process because some tortoises can attempt to bite you and will try to push you away using their shells just to protect their nests. Sulcata tortoises can produce many eggs in a year; the average clutch size is 5 during the breeding season with about 12 to 25 eggs or more. These species really lay lots of eggs which is why sulcatas are abundant in the U.S.

Incubation and Hatching

Once you see that your female had laid eggs, make sure that they're not looking or is far from you when you dig up their eggs. You have to get the eggs and place it in a container for proper incubation and to protect it against potential predation. Incubate the eggs at around 80 to 85 degrees and moistened them with a bit of water. The eggs will usually hatch after 100 to 120 days. Once the hatchlings comes out of the shells, just leave them be in their container until their yolks are fully absorbed, after which you can put the young hatchlings in soft towels until you see their bottom shell is sealed.

Shipping Your Tortoises

The packaging is very important if you're going to ship baby sucata tortoises because you need to make sure that the animals are well protected. You can partner up with other businesses that shipped reptiles so that you can get the lowest rate possible.

The first step is to prepare a box or a normal size cube that measures around 10 x 10 inches. Make sure that the box is quite thick and made up of quality cardboards. Don't forget to print out a sign that says "perishable goods" or "handle with care" and put some arrows in it in red font color so that the delivery man will take care of it during delivery.

The next step is to cut out or buy a Styrofoam that's the same size and shape of your box. The foam inserts has two functions, the first one is that they cushion the package inside and the second one is it insulates the animal from outside temperatures, so that you or your customers won't have to worry about the tortoise getting too cold or whatnot. Just slide the foams on all sides of the box, make sure that they're exactly fitted in the box's size.

After setting up the box, you can buy plastic cups that look like a water dish or sort of a shallow bowl (not the glass cups, more of a delicups). Once you do, just go ahead and put air holes in it using a tool to poke through the cup.

Make a couple of air holes on the plastic cup but not on the box or the foam otherwise it will defeat the purpose of the foam's insulation capabilities because it will let the outside air get inside the box and could make your tortoise uncomfortable during its shipment. You can assure your customers by explaining to them that unlike mammals or humans, tortoises don't breathe as much as we do since they are cold – blooded creatures, so they won't have to worry about the animal not getting enough air inside the box or becoming suffocated because the foams are not air tight, it's only insulated.

Once you've prepared the cup, just tear out a newspaper and crumple it, then put it inside the cup because it will serve as the temporary bedding of the baby tortoise. After doing that, you can go ahead and pick out which baby tortoise is going to go.

Before you do, however, make sure to give them a quick look. Make sure that the tortoise is responsive, has bright and clear eyes, and free of any discharge. Behaviorally speaking, they should be quite scared when getting picked up since they're still babies, they could sort of pull back into their shells – that's actually a good sign that you've properly nursed them.

Make sure that the tortoises are also soaked or hydrated before packing them up because you just never know how long the shipment could take or whatnot, this is just to prepare them for a trip before reaching their new homes. Usually, depending on how far you're going to deliver them, these tortoises are going to be spending around 2 days or more but you don't have to worry about that since they pretty much naturally stay underground as hatchlings.

Once you've checked them out and prepped them up, you can then place them inside the cup, put the lid and close it. After that, place the cup inside the box then just take a couple more shreds of newspapers, crumple them up and place it in the four corners with the cup being the center to prevent it from getting swayed on either sides of the box.

Take a couple more crumpled newspapers and put them on top to provide added security. You can include whatever you want like before you sealed the box, just place some instructions, reminders, a thank you note or some kind of surprise for your customer. You also have to attach a small packaged size heat pad inside the insulated roof (insert it inside the box before completely closing it) to keep the tortoise warm as well.

Once it's all done, just insert the top piece of foam and close the box using a packaging tape to completely seal it. The packaging doesn't have to be pretty but it has to be secure.

Before shipping a tortoise, make sure that you do your research about the particular species because obviously the instructions provided here may only be applicable to grassland tortoises in general like the African sulcata since these species are not aquatic or semi – aquatic like the turtles. Try to also read or research the laws regarding shipping or selling particular tortoise or turtle species because some breeds could be prohibited in being delivered.

Chapter Nine: Common Diseases and Treatments

Tortoises are worth the investment not only because they're generally low maintenance animals and amazing creatures but also because they can live for a very long time which can give hobbyists many years of pet – owning pleasure. The main ingredient in keeping them both happy and healthy is proper care. Like other household pets, they are not immune to diseases or common health issues, you might experience some problems along the way as they grow older but if you are knowledgeable about these potential health threats you can prevent it from happening or be able to handle it effectively so that your tortoises can maximize their health potential.

This chapter will delve deeper on the most common illnesses for sulcata tortoises.

Common Tortoise Diseases, Prevention, and Treatments

Tortoise Prolapses

The small opening (sometimes called cloaca) in a tortoise's scutes just under its tail leading to the animal's reproductive system, the rectal area and the bladder is where prolapse can take place. Prolapse is when the tissues or some part of internal organs comes out through the tortoise's opening.

Unlike most mammals that have water – soluble urea, when these tortoises expel uric acid in the form of urine, it is not water – soluble. It can often time appear as a diluted or concentrated white urine. When this concentrated urea pass through the animal's kidney and the tortoise is always dehydrated or is in a poor diet, this uric acid can become a hard stone in the bladder. Once the body pushes the large and hard stone from the abdominal muscles to the cloaca, it can go up against the soft organs or tissues and instead of the stone being pushed out, the organs, like a male's tortoise's phallus is pushed out instead this is what you call prolapse.

This often time happens among male tortoises, their phallus or penis is where sperm pass through during copulation, so if the phallus is exposed and becomes damaged or dry it won't be able to retract itself back into the shell or the body. When this happens, take your tortoise to the vet as soon as possible.

Vets will try to carefully push the organ inside by applying a hypertonic solution similar to dextrose to draw out the fluid in the swollen penis and shrink it. After that, the phallus will be lubricated and gently be pushed back inside. Vets will then place a suture in the skin of the external opening to stop the organ from coming out until the animal recovers. It will usually take a week or so to fully recover before the sutures are completely removed.

If you bring your pet to the vet as early as you can, it will be much easier to push the organ back to its cloaca but if you don't and the organ becomes too dry, the procedure may not be successful and the phallus could be amputated – which means that the tortoise won't be able to reproduce anymore. Other procedures involve a surgery in the bottom shell of the tortoise to remove the large stones that formed in the bladder; this procedure however, can be very expensive and complicated. Small stones are often treatable through proper hydration so that it can eventually be soluble.

Prolapse can sometimes be caused through mating, because the phallus of the male tortoises are bruised, so make sure to routinely check them every now and then especially if they are housed with female tortoises so that you can separate them to prevent continuous damage to the organ.

Eye Syndrome

One of the more preventable and easily treatable illnesses observed in a tortoise is the eye syndrome. This condition is largely due to improper lighting, hygiene and diet. This is almost always caused by a lack of vitamin A and vitamin D, both of which the animal can get from a proper diet and proper lighting of its habitat.

Shell Rot

Improper diet and lack of calcium are some of the culprits of shell rotting among tortoises and turtles alike. The lack or absence of UVB lighting can cause the shell to slowly degenerate, deteriorate and soften. This can also be cause by lack of calcium which in the long run will weaken its structure and make its bones soft, eventually leading up to the shell.

If your sulcata tortoises displays signs of soft spots, fluid beneath the surface of its plates, oozing pus or discharge, foul smell, shell plates falling off and exposing skin tissue, then that's a clear sign that the shell has rot. You will need to investigate its habitat for the root cause of the fungal or bacterial infection. Too much moisture or too little of it, improper diet, improper heating or lighting and unsanitary conditions are either one or all to blame for shell rot.

A tortoise's shell could also have been scratched, punctured or damaged by a sharp object in the enclosure so ensure that you remove any sharp edged objects and that the whole cage has been cleaned, sanitized, has safe materials, and is kept at the required temperature fit for grassland tortoises needs.

Intestinal Parasites

Parasites and worms find their way into a tortoise's enclosure/tank in a number of ways. To prevent your pet's enclosure in being infested with parasites or other harmful insects, you will want to clean out the enclosure and all its fixtures to make sure there are no left over food or hidden poops that could become a breeding ground for parasites. Scrub down the enclosure and dry out all the cage fixtures before placing them back. Make sure that you have scrubbed all the corners of the enclosure and rinse them off thoroughly.

Make sure to bring your sulcata tortoise to the vet for a quick visit or routine check up to make sure that it is not infested with worms and if this should be the case, to give it the proper treatment it needs before returning it to its enclosure. Thorough cleaning and routine checkup provides a bit of guarantee that parasites won't worsen or spread out to your other collection in the future.

Lung Infections

Lung infections are very common among tortoises like the African sulcata especially if the species came from the wild and were sold illegally from other countries. The shipping of pets from their native land to other countries can put these tortoises under a lot of stress. Factor in the unsanitary living conditions and poor husbandry practices from breeders just trying to make a quick buck off of these pets.

If your pet tortoises are crowdedly packed and shipped in a tight spaced box or enclosure with no food or water during their travel time. Once they arrived, often times, these tortoises and even turtle species already became lethargic, lost some weight and have suffered from respiratory infections.

Of course, if your pet sulcata is kept in captivity and you've bought them from legitimate hobbyists and these breeders raised them in captivity as well, there is lesser chance of them being diagnosed with lung problems. Nevertheless, it is still seen even among captive breeds.

Respiratory diseases can be detected through a physical exam by a reptile vet. You'll also have a clue if your pet will be pre – disposed to this type of illness if you've found out where they came from or how they are raised.

Usually radiographs and blood samples are used to diagnose such disease, and the treatment is antibiotics. The disease can lasts for several weeks and even months depending on how severe the condition is before being treated. Antibiotics and nasal drops can be orally given but most tortoises especially the ill ones often withdraw and hide in their shell which is why the treatment is just injected for easier and faster application.

Most vets will show you how to administer the injection; it's quite easy once you've learned how to do it. These antibiotics will enable your tortoise to clearly smell and tastes its food better.

If the tortoise is already severely ill because of respiratory infections, a feeding tube will be placed and the tortoise will need to undergo surgery to attach the tube on its neck just so the tortoise can eat and recover. It can take several weeks to months until the animal can eat on its own.

Owners can aid their pets during the process by keeping their tortoises warm. Vets will suggest keepers that the tortoises should be kept indoor during treatment and provide them with heat or a full lighting.

Chapter Ten: Care Sheet and Summary

Keeping a sulcata tortoise might look like a piece of cake especially when these creatures are still hatchlings but don't let their starting size fool you because as what all tortoises have proven - it's not about how you start, it's about how you finish! Hopefully, this book has helped you in learning more about this particular species and has guided you in seeing the subtle lessons of keeping a pet tortoise – that life is not a sprint but a marathon, that great things take time, that thinking long – term is always better than short – term, and that keeping a tortoise will teach you the value of true commitment. Have fun in keeping your pet sulcata and long live to both of you!

Biological Information

Taxonomy: Kingdom Animalia, Phylum Chordata, Class Sauropsida, Order Testudines, Family Testudinidae, Genus Centrochelys, Species Sulcata

Distribution and Range: Sahara Desert Africa (specifically in Sahel), Nigeria, Ethiopia, Burkina Faso, Chad, Mali, Mauritania, Sudan, Senegal

Breed Size: 3rd largest tortoise in the world; can grow up to 150 – 200 pounds

Body Type and Appearance: Has furrowed legs and head, has large claws, dull yet thick skin, spiny looking legs and a very sculpted – looking shell

Length: Sulcata Tortoises can grow of up to 33 inches and can reach over 10 inches just within a few years

Weight: They weigh an average of 200 – 250 pounds

Skin Texture: scaly and has a hard sculpted looking shell; its legs are also covered with spiny and dull looking projection

Color: Their top shell has plates that have a shade of yellow, tan or light brown color which are also outlined with brownish colors. Their bottom shell has the same yellowish and tan color.

Temperament: inquisitive, fun, docile, smart, easy to handle and tame, could potentially be aggressive if captured directly in the wild.

Diet: Pure herbivores; they mostly eat plants, grass, flowers, weeds and other green veggies both in the wild and in captivity.

Habitat: Savannahs, Woodlands, Shrublands, Rainforests, and Grasslands

Health Conditions: generally healthy but predisposed to common illnesses such as tortoise prolapse, eye syndrome, lung infection, shell rot and intestinal parasites

Lifespan: average 50 to 80 years

Sulcata Tortoise as Pets

Reminders Before Getting a Sulcata Tortoise

- Keep in mind that these tiny and adorable creatures will grow fast and will require you a lot of your attention and time.
- Make sure that you are ready for some very long term commitment because these pets can probably outlive you

- Keep in mind that it is also illegal to release a tortoise back in the wild. If an individual is caught, one could be heavily fined.
- Think about how many you can handle up to the time that they grow bigger

Behavioral Characteristics in the Wild and in Captivity

- In the wild and even in captivity, sulcata tortoises love to hide and dig large burrows just to get away from the extreme heat of the sun especially for those tortoises living in dryer areas and harsh environments
- African Spur Thigh tortoises are semi – desert to desert species because they are the kind of pets that likes dry environments
- Sulcata tortoises fall under the category of corpuscular; most of the time they're just staying under the burrow waiting for the right time and perfect temperature to come out

Interaction with other Species

- Sulcata tortoises are even-tempered reptiles that could share space with its kind and a few other turtle or younger tortoise species given that they are provided enough room to be housed comfortably.

- If you are planning to house multiple species or sulcata tortoises in one tank, you may need to provide a lot of extra space with many hiding places and visible barriers
- Ensure that all species are fed separately to make sure that each one is properly fed
- No socialization or interaction is needed prior to mixing them however if you may need to quarantine new species to prevent the spread of possible illnesses.

Pros

- Docile, quiet and non – threatening creatures even if it is not trained or socialized
- Requires no supervision, provided that its enclosure is safe and secured
- Keeping them is not that costly and not hard to maintain during its early years

Cons

- Growth may be relatively hard to manage since they can get huge and heavier over time.

- Costs for food, caging and other materials when they reach adulthood could become relatively expensive.
- May not be an ideal pet if you only live in a small house because it needs lots of space as it grows; this pet is ideal for keepers who have a backyard

Tortoise Legalities

- You won't really need to get a license if you decide to keep or breed these adorable creatures because they are listed in the Appendix II of the Convention on International Trade in Endangered Species (CITES) which means that they can be traded for commercial purposes but they can't be taken from the wild

Costs of Keeping a Pet Tortoise

- **Sulcata Tortoise species**: $20 - $80 or more
- **10 to 20 gallon tank/ tortoise table + caging materials** (wood, glass terrarium, plants, water dishes, cage decorations, cleaning materials): more or less $125 (depends on the cage quality)
- **Bedding or Substrate:** $6/bag
- **Heaters/Heat Pads:** around $40
- **Basking Lamp/UVB bulbs:** $30 or more

- **Hiding Spots:** $5 - $10 for hatchlings/juveniles
- **Food:** average of $40 per week for 30 pound bag (prices can vary depending on brand and amount/quantity)
- **Laying bin + additional breeding materials:** $50
- **Total Cost:** more or less $300

Acquiring Sulcata Tortoises

- You would want to acquire a species that is a product of good breeding practices to ensure that they are not sick or doesn't carry other diseases.
- If you have found a healthy and sweet looking sulcata from one of these rescue centers, they could be much cheaper to buy compared to acquiring one from a hobbyist or a legit breeder.
- You also consider acquiring one from a hobbyist either directly or through pet conventions so that you can have more options
- When it comes to purchasing pet tortoises, always buy it from a breeder that is reputable, trustworthy, truly passionate and also a professional

Selecting a Reputable Breeder

- If a breeder lets you walk - through in their facilities to see the conditions and living environment of the animals housed within their site, that's a great indicator of a legit breeder
- Conduct a very simple physical exam to ensure that the species you will get is worth the investment

Selecting a Healthy Tortoise

- Sulcata tortoises should be alert, active and inquisitive.
- They should not appear lethargic and if you give them food, they should at least have an appetite for it.
- Pick up the turtle and determine whether it weighs heavy or light because a light turtle may be ill.
- Scrutinize the top and bottom halves of its shell. They should be sandy or smooth, hard and has yellowish or light brown shaded plates with furrowed but spiny looking legs.
- If the shell is soft once you touch it, this could indicate shell rot.
- Take note of the occurrence of open wounds, discharge from eyes and their interaction with other pets.

Suitable Environment for Sulcata Tortoises

Housing Requirements for Baby Tortoises

- If you want other people to easily view your pet or if you're going to buy a glass terrarium, it's probably better if you black out the rest of the enclosure's sides and only leave one clear side of the glass.
- A wooden tortoise table is ideal especially for land dwellers like the sulcata tortoises because it can save you a few bucks and you can create it in a specification of your choice.
- You can also turn old wooden bookshelves; ensure that it doesn't fall off or have any holes where your baby tortoises can sneak through.
- You can easily purchase a cheap wide plastic tub or mixing tubs (preferably not the clear ones) from your local home depot. These tubs can be a perfect alternative for glass terrariums because they are open.

Caging Materials:

- UVB light
- Heaters/Heat Pad
- Basking Bulb
- Reptibar substrate

- Shallow water dishes
- Food dishes (preferably made out of clay/slightly rough material)
- Misting container
- Small Plastic Enclosure for Soaking
- Hiding Areas (adjust the size as the tortoise grows)
- Sphagnum Moss

Feeding and Nutrition

Nutritional Requirements

- The diet of tortoises in general should be high in fiber and calcium yet low in protein and fruit
- Alfafa hay contains high levels of fiber and calcium but it also contains higher levels of protein than timothy hay
- Make sure that you don't over-feed your pet sulcata with too much alfafa hay
- If you plan to let your pet sulcata graze or if you're picking wild grasses, weeds or other type of vegetation for them to eat, just make sure to offer them fresh produce that are not sprayed with pesticides.

- Plants like collard greens, mustard greens and dandelion greens are all nutritious and packed with high levels of calcium.
- Sulcata tortoises love to eat Dandelion flowers as well as Hibiscus, Rose petals and carnation
- Some vegetables like peas and green beans contain high levels of protein, Iceberg lettuces should also be avoided because it can cause diarrhea to tortoises since it has high water content.
- Fruit can be offered as a treat but make sure that you don't overfeed your pet with it or offer fruits that have high water content
- Sprinkled it with a small amount of calcium supplement preferably with Vitamin D3
- Commercial pellets can also be rotated as part of your pet's diet. You can purchase them through pet stores or online.

Husbandry for Sulcata Tortoise

Building a Tortoise Pen for Adult Sulcatas

- Once they become huge, the best habitat for them is outdoors so that they can also get direct heat from the sun to make them healthy.

- The bigger the pen, the better for your tortoise, this is because it will replicate their habitat in the wild which is much ideal for them.

Ideal Size of the Pen

- The ideal pen size for tortoises in general should be 3 sq. ft. per each inch of its shell.
- Juvenile or growing sulcatas can be housed in a pen that's about 4 x 3 feet in size; adult tortoises should be double or triple than the recommended size.
- You also have to make sure that they are not overcrowded; this is for owners who are considering of keeping more than one sulcata tortoise or housing them with other tortoise or turtle species

How to Build a Play Pen

- Build your pen in a space where your tortoise can have lots of sunshine
- You can also choose to place it in a sort of slope or elevated soil if you have one so that your tortoise can easily turn itself back up if it gets flipped over. If you
- Place it in a spot where it is safe from any hazard or drainage since it can be prone to flooding

Ideal Temperature

- The basking spot should be around 90 degrees Fahrenheit or a bit higher than that since these creatures prefer warmer temperature just like in the desert.
- If you built a green house, the sun can still heat up the enclosure at about 18 degrees Fahrenheit warmer than the cooler temperature outside the green house

Male to Female Tortoise Ratio

- If you house both male and female tortoises together, make sure that the ratio is 1:4 (one male to 4 females)
- Female tortoises get along better than their counterparts, ensure enough space for them
- If you own a couple of male tortoises, you should also make sure to separate them or as much as possible not housed them in one enclosure

How to Protect Tortoises from Predators

- Make sure to supervise your dog or any household pets if you're going to let him mingle with your tortoise and never leave your pet sulcata on its own devises.

- Your tortoise pen should preferably have a fence or a border as well as a rooftop of some sort for added protection against other animals.
- Another common threat for tortoises living outside is pests and insects like fire ants, bees and other poisonous creatures; you can use a bait trap so that these ants will die or use other alternatives. Don't spray pesticides because your tortoise can absorb these chemicals

Handling and Bathing

Proper Handling of Sulcata Tortoise

- You just simply have to grab the bottom and top art of their shell just right in the center using your fingers so that they won't be able to push you off or slide off.
- Don't raise them up too high as they could slip out and fall especially when they get older and stronger.
- Properly hold their shells and apply a tight grip on the center top and bottom.
- Never hold the side of the shells because their rear legs can easily push your finger and they could fall off.

- When your tortoise gets a bit larger and heavier, you should start holding both sides of the top and bottom shell using your hands to provide support.
- Make sure to wash your hands after holding your tortoises because they can potentially have salmonella.
- Try not to put them on their backs and support the shell with both hands.
- Once they become fully grown and if you think you can't lift them up because they're too heavy, it's probably best to let someone help you

How to Bathe Your Tortoise

Bathing Materials:

- Container/Tub
- Water (depends on how big your pet is – just make sure it's not filled up too much)
- Toothbrush
- Cotton Buds
- Towel or dry cloth

- Place your tortoise in the tub and allow it to hydrate himself for about 10 minutes to 20 minutes, after which you can replace the water

- Just gently brush their top shell particularly the areas where dirt can often build up as well as the sides.
- Make sure to clean their scutes and you can also slightly clean their head, legs, neck and tail using cotton buds.
- When brushing their body parts that are not covered with scales or shells, make sure to gently rub it because these areas could be sensitive.
- Clean up their claws thoroughly since this is one of the dirtiest parts of your tortoise's body as well as the bottom shell or the plastron
- Once you're done removing the dirt, you can now rinse them with water.
- Don't use any unnecessary product (unless recommended by your vet) because it can be fatal for some tortoise.
- After you have rinsed them off, take them out of the water, and dry them up using a soft towel or cloth.
- Gently do this at least once or twice a week or even once a month so that your tortoise can be nice and clean.

Breeding and Shipping Tortoises

Sexual Dimorphism

- Males have concave bottom shells with thicker and longer tales.
- Females are relatively smaller than male sulcatas and their anal scutes in their plastron have a much smaller opening than that of the males.

Nesting

- Nesting usually happens around 6 to 8 weeks after copulation, you'll know this when you see your female sulcata digging holes using its front legs.
- Once they complete their digging process, the female excavates their egg chamber and starts laying eggs.
- During this time, some female sulcatas can also become overly aggressive if they found out that people or other species are near their nests.
- The average clutch size is 5 during the breeding season with about 12 to 25 eggs or more

Incubation and Hatching

- Incubate the eggs at around 80 to 85 degrees and moistened them with a bit of water. The eggs will usually hatch after 100 to 120 days.

- Once the hatchlings comes out of the shells, just leave them be in their container until their yolks are fully absorbed

- Put the young hatchlings in soft towels until you see their bottom shell is sealed

Shipping Your Tortoises

- Prepare a box or a normal size cube that measures around 10 x 10 inches.
- Make sure that the box is quite thick and made up of quality cardboards.
- Don't forget to print out a sign that says "perishable goods" or "handle with care"
- Cut out or buy a Styrofoam that's the same size and shape of your box.
- After setting up the box, you can buy plastic cups that look like a water dish or sort of a shallow bowl
- Make a couple of air holes on the plastic cup but not on the box or the foam otherwise it will defeat the purpose of the foam's insulation capabilities

- Tear out a newspaper and crumple it then put it inside the cup because it will serve as the temporary bedding then pick out which baby tortoise is going to go.
- Make sure that the tortoises are also soaked or hydrated before packing them up; place them inside the cup, put the lid and close it
- Place the cup inside the box then just take a couple more shreds of newspapers, crumple them up and place it in the four corners
- Take a couple more crumpled newspapers and put them on top to provide added security.
- Attach a small packaged size heat pad inside the insulated roof (insert it inside the box before completely closing it) to keep the tortoise warm
- Once it's all done, just insert the top piece of foam and close the box using a packaging tape to completely seal it.

Common Diseases and Treatments

Tortoise Prolapses: Prolapse is when the tissues or some part of internal organs comes out through the tortoise's opening.

Eye Syndrome: It is caused by a lack of vitamin A and vitamin D, both of which the animal can get from a proper diet and proper lighting of its habitat.

Shell Rot: The lack or absence of UVB lighting can cause the shell to slowly degenerate, deteriorate and soften eventually leading up to the shell.

Intestinal Parasites: Thorough cleaning and routine checkup provides a bit of guarantee that parasites won't worsen or spread out to your other collection in the future

Lung Infections: The shipping of pets from their native land to other countries can put these tortoises under a lot of stress. Unsanitary living conditions and poor husbandry practices can cause lung infections

Glossary

Acclimation – Adjusting to a new environment or new
conditions over a period of time

Acrylic Aquarium – Glass aquarium alternative, usually
lighter than an ordinary aquarium but can be easily
scratched.

Active range – The area of activity which can include
hunting, seeking refuge, and finding a mate

Ambient temperature – The overall temperature of the
environment

Amelanistic – Amel for short; without melanin, or without
any black or brown coloration.

Ammonia – made up of nitrogen and hydrogen. It has an
unpleasant smell that's also toxic and corrosive. Leftover
food in the enclosure can be contributing factors that build
up ammonia

Anerythristic – Anery for short; without any red coloration.

Aquatic – Lives in water.

Arboreal – Lives in trees.

Bacteria – microorganisms that are distributed widely in the
environments. Tortoise keepers should be aware of the
harmful effects of bacteria

Bacteria Bloom – sometimes referred to as a tank syndrome.

Basking – a procedure where tortoises or turtles warms or dries up their body. Tortoises will need to have a basking area at a certain temperature to prevent shell rot. It also allows absorption of UVA and UVB for thermoregulation Betadine – An antiseptic that can be used to clean wounds in reptiles

Bilateral – Where stripes, spots or markings are present on both sides of an animal.

Biotic – The living components of an environment.

Bridge – part of the shell that's located in the middle of the front and black legs connecting the top and bottom shell.

Brumation – The equivalent of mammalian hibernation among reptiles

Cannibalistic – Where an animal feeds on others of its own kind.

Cloaca – also vent; a half-moon shaped opening for digestive waste disposal and sexual organs.

Cloacal Gaping – Indication of sexual receptivity of the female.

Cloacal Gland – A gland at the base of the tail which emits foul smelling liquid as a defense mechanism; also called Anal Gland.

Clutch – A batch of eggs.

Constriction – The act of wrapping or coiling around a prey to subdue and kill it prior to eating.

Crepuscular – Active at twilight, usually from dusk to dawn.

Diurnal – Active by day

Drop – To lay eggs or to bear live young

Ectothermic – Cold-blooded. An animal that cannot regulate its own body temperature, but sources body heat from the surroundings

Endemic – Indigenous to a specific region or area.

Estivation – Also Aestivation; a period of dormancy that usually occurs during the hot or dry seasons in order to escape the heat or to remain hydrated.

Flexarium – A reptile enclosure that is mostly made from mesh screening, for species that require plenty of ventilation.

Fossorial – A burrowing species.

Gestation – The period of development of an embryo within a female.

Gravid – The equivalent of pregnant in reptiles

Gut-loading – Feeding insects within 24 hours to a prey before they are fed to your pet, so that they pass on the nutritional benefits

Hatchling – A newly hatched, or baby, reptile.

Herps/Herpetiles – A collective name for reptile and amphibian species.

Herpetoculturist – A person who keeps and breeds reptiles in captivity

Herpetologist – A person who studies ectothermic animals, sometimes also used for those who keeps reptiles.

Herpetology – The study of reptiles and amphibians.

Hide Box – A furnishing within a reptile cage that gives the animal a secure place to hide.

Husbandry – The daily care of a pet reptile.

Hygrometer – Used to measure humidity.

Impaction – A blockage in the digestive tract due to the swallowing of an object that cannot be digested or broken down.

Incubate – Maintaining eggs in conditions favorable for development and hatching.

Juvenile – Not yet adult; not of breedable age

LTC – Long Term Captive; or one that has been in captivity for more than six months.

MBD – Metabolic Bone Disease; occurs when reptiles lack sufficient calcium in their diet.

Morph – Color pattern

Musking – Secretion of a foul smelling liquid from its vent as a defense mechanism.

Oviparous – Egg-bearing.

Ovoviviparous – Eggs are retained inside the female's body until they hatch.

Popping – The process by which the sex is determined among hatchlings.

Probing – The process by which the sex is determined among adults.

Sloughing – Shedding.

Sub-adult – Juvenile

Substrate – The material lining the bottom of a reptile enclosure.

Stat – Short for Thermostat

Tag – Slang for a bite or being bitten

Terrarium – A reptile enclosure.

Thermo-regulation – The process by which cold-blooded animals regulate their body temperature by moving from hot to cold surroundings.

Vent – Cloaca

Vivarium – Glass-fronted enclosure

Viviparous – Gives birth to live young.

WC – Wild Caught

WF – Wild Farmed; refers to the collection of a pregnant female whose eggs or young were hatched or born in captivity.

Yearling – A year old.

Zoonosis – A disease that can be passed from animal to man.

Photo Credits

Page 1 Photo by user Jean Rebiffé via Flickr.com,
https://www.flickr.com/photos/jeanot/17148096955/

Page 3 Photo by user Jared Lindsay via Flickr.com,
https://www.flickr.com/photos/cinder6/4460185249/

Page 9 Photo by user D Coetzee via Flickr.com,
https://www.flickr.com/photos/dcoetzee/4788716045/

Page 25 Photo by user Tjflex2 via Flickr.com,
https://www.flickr.com/photos/tjflex/32371120145/

Page 34 Photo by user Rodney Lewis via Flickr.com,
https://www.flickr.com/photos/70172955@N00/7882121434/

Page 43 Photo by user BrandonLord via Flickr.com,
https://www.flickr.com/photos/95508982@N06/11595546885/

Page 49Photo by user Paul Morris via Flickr.com,
https://www.flickr.com/photos/aa3sd/7360055076/

Page 57 Photo by user liesvanrompaey via Flickr.com,
https://www.flickr.com/photos/liesvanrompaey/4841630599/

References

African Spurred Tortoise - Wikipedia.org

https://en.wikipedia.org/wiki/African_spurred_tortoise

African Spurred Tortoise - SanDiegoZoo.org
http://animals.sandiegozoo.org/animals/african-spurred-
tortoise

African Sulcata Tortoise: Species Profile: Housing, Diet, and
Care - PetEducation.com

http://www.peteducation.com/article.cfm?c=17+1797&aid=24
34

Basic care: Sulcata Tortoise - Azeah.com

http://azeah.com/tortoises-turtles/basic-care-sulcata-tortoise

Breeding and Incubation - TheTortoiseShop.com

https://www.thetortoiseshop.com/tortoise-breeding-
incubation

Building an Outdoor Habitat for a Sulcata Tortoise -
Pethelpful.com

https://pethelpful.com/reptiles-amphibians/housing-a-
sulcata-tortoise

Captive Desert Tortoise Health and Illnesses - Azgfd.com

https://www.azgfd.com/wildlife/nongamemanagement/tortoise/health/

Creating an Outdoor Sulcata Tortoise Pen - BackWaterReptilesBlog.com

http://backwaterreptilesblog.com/creating-outdoor-sulcata-tortoise-pen/

Everything You Need to Know About Raising a Sulcata Tortoise - Pethelpful.com

https://pethelpful.com/reptiles-amphibians/sulcata-tortoises

How to Bathe a Tortoise - Cuteness.com

https://www.cuteness.com/article/bathe-tortoise

How to Care for a Tortoise - HowToCareforaTortoise.com

http://www.howtocareforatortoise.com/tortoise-diet-2/

Housing Tortoises Indoors - Ideas for Building Custom Enclosures - TheSpruce.com

https://www.thespruce.com/ideas-for-buildling-custom-tortoise-enclosures-1239546

Nesting & Egg Laying In a Group of African Sulcata Tortoises - TigerHomes.org

http://www.tigerhomes.org/animal/egg-laying-sulcata-tortoises.cfm

Shipping a Tortoise - TheReptileReport.com

http://thereptilereport.com/shipping-a-tortoise-2/

Shipping a turtle or tortoise - TurtleRescues.com

http://www.turtlerescues.com/shipping_turtles.htm

Should I give my Tortoise a Bath? - TortoiseTrust.org

https://www.tortoisetrust.org/articles/bath.html

Three Common Ailments of Tortoises in Captivity
ReptilesMagazine.com

http://www.reptilesmagazine.com/Reptile-Health/Disease-Management/Three-Common-Ailments-Of-Tortoises-In-Captivity/

Feeding Baby
Cynthia Cherry
978-1941070000

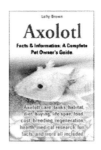

Axolotl
Lolly Brown
978-0989658430

Dysautonomia, POTS
Syndrome
Frederick Earlstein
978-0989658485

Degenerative Disc
Disease Explained
Frederick Earlstein
978-0989658485

Sinusitis, Hay Fever,
Allergic Rhinitis Explained
Frederick Earlstein
978-1941070024

Wicca
Riley Star
978-1941070130

Zombie Apocalypse
Rex Cutty
978-1941070154

Capybara
Lolly Brown
978-1941070062

Eels As Pets
Lolly Brown
978-1941070167

Scabies and Lice Explained
Frederick Earlstein
978-1941070017

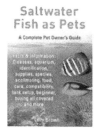

Saltwater Fish As Pets
Lolly Brown
978-0989658461

Torticollis Explained
Frederick Earlstein
978-1941070055

Kennel Cough
Lolly Brown
978-0989658409

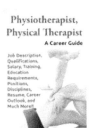

Physiotherapist, Physical
Therapist
Christopher Wright
978-0989658492

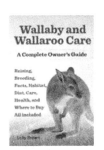

Rats, Mice, and Dormice
As Pets
Lolly Brown
978-1941070079

Wallaby and Wallaroo Care
Lolly Brown
978-1941070031

Bodybuilding Supplements
Explained
Jon Shelton
978-1941070239

Demonology
Riley Star
978-19401070314

Pigeon Racing
Lolly Brown
978-1941070307

Dwarf Hamster
Lolly Brown
978-1941070390

Cryptozoology
Rex Cutty
978-1941070406

Eye Strain
Frederick Earlstein
978-1941070369

Inez The Miniature Elephant
Asher Ray
978-1941070353

Vampire Apocalypse
Rex Cutty
978-1941070321

Made in the USA
Las Vegas, NV
05 March 2024

86751792R00075